Family Crises

Jillian Powell

WAYLAND

First published in 2008
by Wayland

Copyright © Wayland 2008

Wayland
Hachette Children's Books
338 Euston Road
London NW1 3BH

Wayland Australia
Level 17/207 Kent Street
Sydney, NSW 2000

Series editor: Nicola Edwards
Consultant: Peter Evans
Designer: Alix Wood
Picture researcher: Kathy Lockley

The author and publisher would like to thank the following for allowing their pictures to be reproduced in this publication:
ClassicStock/H. Armstrong Roberts/Alamy: 4; Ned Frisk Photography/Corbis: 5
Nick Kennedy/Alamy: 7; Joanne O'Brien/Photofusion: 18; Photodisc/SW Productions/Alamy: Cover, 10; Paula Solloway/Photofusion: 6; Wishlist: Title page, 8, 9, 11-17, 20-45; Wolf/zefa/Corbis:19

British Library Cataloguing in Publication Data

Powell, Jillian
    Family crises. - (Emotional health issues)
    1. Problem families - Juvenile literature
    I. Title
    362.8'2

ISBN 978 0 7502 4911 9

Printed in China

Wayland is a division of Hachette Children's Books,
an Hachette Livre UK company.

The case studies in this book are based on real experiences but the names we have used are fictitious and do not relate to real people. Except where a caption of a photograph specifically names a person appearing in that photograph, all the people we have featured in the book are models.

Contents

Words that appear in **bold** can be found in the glossary on page 46.

Introduction

Josh is running away. It is not the first time Josh has left home, but this time he intends to stay away. Things began to go wrong when his dad left home when Josh was eleven. Josh always seemed to be arguing with his mum and it got much worse when her new partner Greg moved in. Greg **bullies** Josh and has even threatened him with violence. Josh once saw Greg hit his mum too, but she still let him stay. She doesn't seem to care if Josh stays or not, so he has decided to leave. His family is in crisis.

Changes in the family

Families are changing. Two **generations** ago, most children lived in families with two parents. Today there are many more kinds of family. Single-parent families and **blended** or stepfamilies are becoming more common. Single parents may be divorced or separated or may never have married. Blended families result when one or both parents find new partners. Some children are brought up by two parents of the same sex. Others are brought up by grandparents or in **foster families** or are **adopted** into new families.

Blended families

If a parent is divorced or **bereaved** and remarries, children may have to adjust to living with a stepparent and step-siblings. Sometimes, this can be hard.

An image of traditional family life. In the 1950s and 1960s, most family units were two married parents living with their children.

They may resent a stepparent taking their natural parent's place, or they may feel jealous of them. They may be jealous of their new step-siblings, too. Children may feel guilty about being part of a stepfamily if their other parent is alone. It can also be hard adjusting to another family's ways of doing things, and there can be disagreements, especially when step-siblings have to share rooms and belongings.

Although some children settle and adjust, others may go on feeling unhappy and lonely. This can lead to **depression** and stress-related illnesses that affect their home and school life.

Impact on children

Many children experience change and upheaval as they are growing up. They can face family crises that challenge their physical and mental wellbeing. Rising cases of childhood depression and emotional, mental and behavioural disorders reflect increasing stresses in family life today.

Find out more

This book gives you the facts about family crises. It explains the

circumstances and events that can cause stress, conflict and unhappiness within families and the impact they have on young people's feelings and lives. It gives advice on support and provides information about available resources. The book also shows that people can overcome problems and find ways to survive and recover from family crises.

Many children today grow up in single parent families.

5

Chapter 1: *Changing lifestyles*

As well as changes to the family unit, there have been huge social changes in the last few decades. Fifty years ago, most people stayed and worked in the area where they were born. **Extended families** (grandparents, uncles and aunts) were often close at hand to provide support, advice and childcare. Today, people are more mobile, often moving away to live and work. This has meant the loss of traditional family support systems. Once, young parents could turn to their own parents or grandparents for help and advice. Now they may live a long way away, or they may have lost contact with their families.

Work and childcare

Family lifestyles have also changed greatly in recent decades. In the past, most women stayed at home to look after young children, while their husbands were the 'breadwinners', going out to work to earn money. Today, people's working patterns have changed. In some families, the mother is the wage earner and her partner is the 'house husband', looking after the home and family. In many families, both parents go out to work and this may mean they have less time to spend with children as a

Children with working parents may have to rely on meals heated up in a microwave if their parents are busy.

family. They may rely on grandparents, nannies or babysitters, day-care centres or after-school clubs for childcare.

Fast-food meals

Eating habits have also changed. Few families now sit down round a table for regular meals. In the past, breakfast was the start of a family day. Today, many children grab a sandwich or cereal bar on the way to school. In the evenings, they may eat in front of the television rather than seated round a table, discussing the day.

In focus: the impact of technology

Technology has changed family life, so that family members spend less time interacting with and talking to one another. For example, when televisions first came into family homes in the 1950s, families sat round together to watch favourite shows. Today many children have their own TV sets and watch alone in their bedrooms.

Children may also spend time at home playing on handheld video games or computers, texting their friends on mobile phones or listening to music through headphones, while their parents use the Internet or watch television in another room.

These changes in work and life patterns mean that the members of a family live more separate lives than used to be the case. When a crisis occurs, such as an illness, a **bereavement** or relationship problems, it can be harder for families to work things out together.

For many families, watching TV is no longer a shared activity. Children may have TV sets in their bedrooms and watch the same programme separately from other family members.

Chapter 2: *Family breakup*

Family breakup happens when parents decide to separate or divorce. Divorce is one of the most stressful events a family can experience. It affects every member of the family – parents, children, grandparents and other close relatives.

Life changes

Since laws have changed, making it much easier for couples to divorce, family breakup has become much more common. Many couples decide to split because they no longer love each other or because they have grown apart and want different things from life. Some meet new partners and decide to move in with them.

When this happens, their children face huge life changes. Parents have to decide, sometimes with the help of the court, who will have **custody** of the children. Some children will live part of the time with one parent, part with the other. Some will live mainly with one parent and visit the other regularly. Some may see the absent parent only occasionally, or not at all.

After a split, children have to adapt to new routines, such as spending one weekend with one parent and the next with the other.

If parents move away, children may rely on contact by email, phone or post.

While many parents co-operate with one another after divorce, some are hostile. This can mean that children lose contact with grandparents and other relatives from one side of the family. This can be difficult for everyone involved. In extreme cases, a parent who has been denied custody may illegally take a child away to live with him or her.

One or both parents may find new partners and re-marry. If they do so, the children have to adjust to a 'blended' family, living part-time or full-time with a new stepparent and sometimes step-siblings. When families break up, it can mean a move for one or both parents to a new house or even to a new neighbourhood, so children may need to change schools and find new friends, bringing more change and upheaval. All this can be stressful for everyone in the family.

It's a fact: marriage and divorce

- There are around 150,000 divorces each year in the UK.
- Almost two in three marriages end in divorce.
- Half of all divorces involve children under the age of 16.
- **Co-habiting** couples are more likely to split up than married couples.
- One in ten families is a stepfamily.

The impact of family breakup

Family breakup can be a tense and uncomfortable time for all. A couple may argue constantly or may not talk to each other at all. They may often be stressed and irritable, snapping at others about things that would not normally bother them.

Some children hear their parents saying hurtful things or even witness violence between them. The children may feel afraid for a parent's safety, and for themselves and their siblings.

Taking the blame

This is a worrying and confusing time for children. Often they do not understand why their parents cannot get along as they used to. Children may believe that the family breakup is somehow their fault – that it is the result of something they have done or not done. They may hope that they can prevent their parents from breaking up.

Children may worry about where they will live and whether they will see a parent who is moving out of the family home. Children are sometimes forced to 'take sides' with one parent

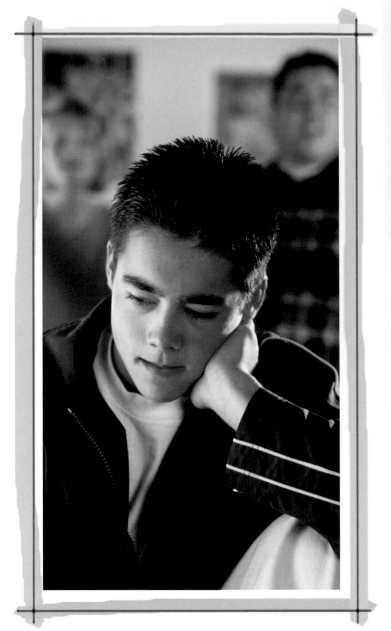

Arguments and conflict can make children feel torn and confused.

against the other, which complicates their feelings of hurt and confusion.

Experiencing loss

Children can experience many difficult emotions during a family breakup – sadness, anger, **anxiety**, fear and embarrassment. There is often an overwhelming sense of loss and a yearning for how things used to be in the family.

A child may find it hard to concentrate in class or do homework because he or she is worried about what is going on at home and what will happen in the future. These worries and distractions can have a negative effect on a child's performance at school. Parents may notice that children's grades slide after a separation or divorce, though they usually improve once things have settled down.

Concentration on school work is difficult when a child's emotions are in turmoil.

CASE STUDY

Dawn's parents were always arguing. Dawn used to hear them when she had gone to bed. Sometimes she sat on the stairs and cried because she felt so worried. Their voices were always so angry and upset. One day her parents told Dawn and her sister that they no longer loved each other and they were getting a divorce. Her dad moved out the next weekend. Dawn felt heartbroken. She hated the fights, but she didn't want her dad to leave. She desperately hoped her mum and dad would get back together again. It felt worse on special days, like her birthday and Christmas, when she didn't even get to see her dad, although he phoned in the evening. Dawn tried to think of ways to get her dad to spend time with her mum again, but then she found out that he was in a relationship with another woman. Dawn knew that, however much she wanted it, her parents would never get back together again. The only thing that helped was chatting to her friend Ellie, because Ellie had gone through the same thing two years earlier. Ellie told Dawn that things would get better in time.

Working things through

Children aren't always able to talk openly about how they feel during a family breakup. They may be worried that they will cause more trouble and anger between their parents. Young people may be put under pressure to 'take sides' in a parental conflict. They may feel anxious about upsetting or disappointing one parent. Some children feel angry and let down by their parents, and react by withdrawing from them in their mind and their daily lives.

Depression

Many children experience anxiety and depression during and after their parents' breakup. Depression can be the result of feeling powerless to change or control the situation.

Children may feel particularly upset on special occasions such as birthdays, holidays, or other family celebrations.

Teachers may offer understanding and support if they are aware of what is happening during a family crisis at home.

They may experience behavioural problems and their conduct at school may suffer.

Talking therapies

Children need to talk about how they feel if they are to come to terms with family breakup. They need to discuss what is happening with their parents and describe how it is affecting them. Young people can talk to teachers or school **counsellors** who will understand what the students are going through and why their schoolwork may be affected.

Some children may need to meet with a child or family counsellor, a **therapist** or a **social worker**. These

Support groups offer a safe place where children can express their emotions and feel that they are less alone with their problems.

can help children work out their emotions and make better sense of their situation. At divorce recovery support groups, children can meet with others who are experiencing the same problems and feelings. They can also get advice and support from telephone helplines.

Coping strategies

There are strategies that can help children cope. These include keeping to familiar routines, especially in arrangements for seeing absent parents. Maintaining contact with other relatives, such as grandparents, and with family pets can provide stability and comfort.

Keeping a diary may help children to express their feelings freely. Physical exercise relieves stress because it produces **endorphins** in the brain that help to counteract depression. Trying new activities or sports can be a distraction and can help children feel excitement about new things, not just despair about loss.

In focus: child custody

Some parents agree on arrangements for child custody between them. But if they can't agree, they may need to go to court, where a judge decides. A children's or family court reporter may talk to children and their parents to find out how they feel, then report to the court.

Children are never asked to choose between parents, but when they are asked what they want to happen, they may have divided loyalties, and be concerned that their decision will upset one of their parents. They may need to be assured that they will go on seeing the absent parent and that their relationship will stay the same, whatever the living arrangements.

Chapter 3: *Bereavement*

The death of a loved one is one of the hardest things anyone can face. Bereavement can bring deep sadness, an aching sense of loss, and a feeling of being abandoned. Grief is a normal and natural response to loss. If someone has died suddenly, perhaps from a heart attack or in a traffic accident, shock and disbelief are natural reactions. When there has been no time for goodbyes, children sometimes feel guilty about things said or not said, or about their recent behaviour. Guilt may be felt more keenly where a parent or sibling has died by suicide. If there has been a **terminal illness**, a long period of stress and anxiety may have preceded the death. During times like this, children may have missed out on normal family life and fun or have had to be more self-sufficient because of the family situation.

Feeling isolated

Children who have lost a parent or a sibling can feel very isolated. They may not know others who have been bereaved in the same way. They may feel awkward or embarrassed among their peers because they are 'different'. They may believe that nobody can understand how they are feeling. Some children may have to face taunts or difficult questions about what has happened to them. Friends who are uncomfortable or who don't know what to say may avoid the bereaved person.

Children who have been bereaved can feel isolated from their friends as they may think that no-one understands what they are experiencing.

Coping with emotions

Many children struggle bravely to cope when they are hurting inside. They may put on a brave face because they don't want to cause a grieving parent more worry. Young people may feel resentful about how their family life has been affected. They may believe that there is little point in doing schoolwork or any of the activities they used to enjoy.

The loss of a close relative can leave young people feeling anxious about their own death, or that of a relative. Some children experience physical symptoms, such as aches and pains. Teens may become withdrawn and more likely to take risks with alcohol, drugs or sex as a reaction to what has happened.

For some people, the feelings of shock, distress and bitterness surrounding their loved one's death may persist for many months, making them feel severely depressed. They may be unable to see anything positive about the future. Through counselling and therapy, these people can be helped to come to terms with their grief and move on with their lives.

It's a fact: bereavement

- Every hour in the UK, two children under 16, or 20,000 children a year, are bereaved of a parent.
- 5 per cent of children aged between five and 15 have experienced the death of a parent or sibling.
- 10 per cent of five to 15 year-olds (over one million children) have experienced the death of a close relative, carer or friend.
- The most common causes of bereavement are cancer, suicide, heart problems and road traffic accidents.

Children often have a special bond with their grandparents. Losing a grandparent may be a child's first experience of bereavement.

Coping with change

The death of a parent can bring many changes to a child's life. Some children continue to live with the surviving parent, sometimes with the help of additional childcare; some may be cared for by grandparents or other close relatives. When a parent or a sibling dies, children often feel that their role within the family has changed. A son who loses his father, for example, may feel he is now the 'man of the house'.

The death of a sibling also brings changes in family relationships. Children may have difficult and confused feelings, such as guilt that they are alive when their parents are mourning the sibling. Children who lose a sibling may initially feel resentment, followed by shame or guilt.

Losing a grandparent is painful for many children. Often it can be like losing a trusted adviser, someone who was 'on their side' and who would always listen to them. For many children, the loss of a

Some children act as carers for younger siblings when their parent dies. For example, if her mother has died, a daughter may feel that she has to take on responsibility for looking after younger members of the family.

grandparent can be the first experience of death. If a grandparent has been ill, there may be an element of relief at

16

the end of suffering, but that in turn can bring feelings of guilt.

Children and teens can also be deeply affected by the death of a close friend. If a friend dies, for example from an illness or an accident, this can leave young people feeling insecure and anxious, particularly if they are of a similar age.

A pet's death can cause strong and painful feelings too, as pets are often an important part of the family, and their loss can leave a huge gap in a young person's life.

CASE STUDY

Jake was nine when his father died suddenly from a heart attack. Jake remembers that a teacher took him out of class to tell him the news. Jake felt as if his whole world had fallen apart. His dad had seemed so fit, and they often played football together. Jake's sister was too young to understand, and Jake felt it was up to him now to look after his mum. He couldn't bear to see her sad, and he worried that she would become ill or that something bad would happen to her. Jake tried to hold things together for his mum, but he often cried himself to sleep.

Jake's teacher noticed Jake's distress and talked to his mother. She arranged for him to go on a residential weekend where he would meet other children who had lost a parent. At first Jake found it hard to talk about his dad, but when he listened to the other children there, he realized they would understand. It helped a lot knowing others were going through the same emotions.

Some people find it comforting to visit the grave of a loved one. Often this is the place where they feel able to talk to the person they have lost.

Healing and recovery

Many people need extra help and support to help them cope following a bereavement. When someone dies suddenly, families often receive immediate support from hospitals or police **family liaison officers**. Hospitals and **hospices** can give support where a death has been expected due to illness.

Many people find that in the immediate aftermath of a death, they feel a numbness that helps them cope with the many tasks that have to be done. They may have immediate support from family, friends and neighbours as they inform people and make arrangements for funerals.

It is often later, when the funeral is over and people have returned to their normal routines, that families struggle to cope with loss. They may feel that others expect them to get better and show signs of recovery. People may find it difficult to talk to them about their loss, especially if the death was by suicide. But talking is an important part of healing.

Talking as therapy

Children can sometimes feel afraid that they will forget their loved one. It is important that they have the chance to remember the person, talk about him or her, and express their feelings. If they are finding it hard, teachers, doctors, youth workers and family liaison officers can all play an important role in listening and providing information and support.

Some schools may arrange for students to have access to a counsellor during the school day and allow them to be excused from classes for counselling sessions.

In schools, counsellors can provide an outlet for children when emotions build up during the day.

Goodbye ceremonies, such as releasing a balloon for the person who has died, can be an important part of the healing process for children who have been bereaved.

Counselling and support groups

Bereavement organizations offer individual counselling as well as support groups, where people who have lost a loved one can meet others who are experiencing the same difficult emotions.

Residential courses are also available to children who have been bereaved. They provide a safe and comfortable environment in which children can talk about what has happened and how they feel. Meeting other children who have gone through similar experiences and finding out they are not alone can change a child's perspective on what has happened.

Such programmes aim to rebuild a child's **self-esteem**, which can be damaged by the loss of feelings of security, trust, and control that bereavement can cause.

In focus: *healing and recovery*

In the UK, the charity Winston's Wish organises residential weekends for children who have been bereaved. Children take part in activities such as the 'Wilderness Challenge', which includes a night walk and candlelit ceremony around a campfire. Courses include activities such as making a memory book to remind them of their loved one, expressing their feelings of anger and resentment on an 'anger wall' and goodbye ceremonies, such as releasing balloons or lighting candles.

19

Chapter 4: *Illness and disability*

Young carers are children who look after someone in their family who has an illness, a disability or a problem with drug or alcohol abuse. The rise in the number of one-parent families means that more children are having to care for an ill or a disabled parent and, sometimes, younger siblings. Some children have to help care for a brother or sister who is ill or disabled. Most young carers are aged between eight and 15 years, although some are as young as five. They take on responsibilities for caring for someone in a practical or emotional way that would normally fall to an adult.

Physical and emotional care

Young carers may have to do household jobs, such as cooking and cleaning, while also giving physical care, including helping a family member get dressed, feeding and bathing the person, and giving **medication**. Care may involve the heavy lifting of someone who is physically disabled. It can also mean giving emotional support to someone with a mental illness, such as depression. A young carer may need to help someone cope with a drug or alcohol **addiction**. This can be especially hard for children, as

Supporting a parent with mental health or addiction problems can be emotionally draining for a young person.

damaging their things. They may also have to look after themselves most of the time, because their sibling takes up so much of their parents' time and attention.

Coping with crises

Some children may have to deal with upsetting and challenging situations, such as coping with a parent who is in severe pain or one who has been **binge drinking** or has taken a drug overdose. These situations put children under a great deal of emotional and physical strain.

Many young carers juggle school work with responsibilities at home, such as domestic tasks and looking after younger siblings.

they often find it difficult to talk to others about the problems at home.

Caring for siblings

Children who have an ill or disabled brother or sister may have to stay at home often to keep an eye on them, or spend time helping with feeding, bathing and caring for them. Sometimes they may have to cope with difficult behaviour, such as siblings misbehaving in public or

It's a fact: young carers

- There are an estimated 175,000 young carers in the UK.
- Around 7 per cent of young carers spend more than 50 hours a week caring.
- Around two-thirds of young carers care for someone with a physical disability.
- Around a third care for someone with a mental health problem.

21

Problems faced by young carers

Children who are full-time carers often worry about the future and what will happen if their parent or sibling dies. It can be hard for them to leave the person they care for and take time out for themselves because they feel worried or guilty when they do. They may feel angry or resentful about their role as caregiver and may think that others do not appreciate what they do. This, in turn, can cause feelings of guilt.

Coping alone

Young carers have to deal with many problems alone, such as stress, worry, fatigue and lack of time to spend with

Young carers may spend a lot more time indoors than other young people of the same age. They may envy their friends because they may appear to have much more freedom and to enjoy more carefree lifestyles.

peers or engage in social and recreational activities. Problems such as these can lead to depression and even to **self-harm**. Self-harm can be a young carer's response to feeling that they have no control over their life, or that no one is listening to them.

Many young carers also suffer problems with their physical health, such as tiredness from having to get up during the night, or back injuries

CASE STUDY

Sarah was eight when she realised how sick her mum was. She started helping around the house, doing the dishes, cooking meals and looking after her younger brother Sam and sister Natasha. Her mum's **arthritis** became so bad it made it hard to get around. Sarah got up early every day to make breakfast and help dress Sam and Natasha. Before she went to school, she had to make sure that her mum had her medication. After school, Sarah had to pick up Sam and Natasha, then make a meal when they got home. She had to clean up the house before doing her homework and make sure the little ones got ready for bed. Sarah was often really tired at school, but she didn't like making a fuss because she didn't want others to feel she was different or feel sorry for her. She missed a lot of school and dropped out when she was sixteen.

from lifting a parent in and out of a bed or bath.

School and education

Surveys have found that as many as one in three young carers has problems at school. Getting to school on time and participating in after-school activities can be hard. Some students miss school because a parent has asked them to stay home or because they are worried about leaving a parent alone.

Young carers may have to get up extra early and go to bed late because of all the additional domestic tasks such as cleaning and washing up that they have to fit into their day.

Parents with problems

Some children have to act as carers because their parents are going through problems which leave them unable to cope with caring for a home and family. Some parents are addicted to drugs or alcohol; others may have a problem with gambling. Families may not want others to know about the addiction, and it becomes a family 'secret' that a child is sworn to keep. Addictions can even cause a parent to turn to crime to pay for a habit. The effects on a family can be devastating. Debt can cause parents to fall behind with rent or mortgage payments and lose a home or be evicted. Crime can result in an arrest, conviction and time in prison.

Feeling isolated

These problems are hard to talk about, and children often feel embarrassed or ashamed to tell others what is happening at home. They may have problems concentrating at school or getting homework done. They may have feelings of isolation and **stigma**, and some may have to put up with bullying and hurtful remarks about their family from other children. They may also feel confused because they have been hurt, disappointed or betrayed by a parent whom they love and need.

Coping with crises

Children should not have to cope alone with situations like this. Alcohol and drugs can alter behaviour and lead to parents taking dangerous risks or behaving in an irrational, angry or aggressive way. A parent may take a **drug overdose**, accidentally or intentionally, or drink so heavily that he or she loses consciousness. In these circumstances, children need to call emergency service providers, such as police or **paramedics**. The child should always stay on the line until help arrives.

Some young carers have to cope with bullying and taunts from thoughtless peers.

If a parent blacks out or tries to commit suicide, the emergency services will offer instant advice and help, and will stay on the line until an ambulance crew arrives on the scene.

As well as practical help, children whose parents have problems also need the emotional support of talking to others. They should try to talk to someone they trust so that other adults understand what is happening at home and can support them.

If they do not feel able to approach anyone in person, they can call a helpline for immediate advice and support. Some organizations specialize in helping children whose parents have addiction problems.

It's a fact:
parents with problems

- One in 25 parents in the UK has an alcohol problem.
- Over a million children in the UK have a parent with an alcohol problem.
- Half of all **domestic violence** cases occur where parents have an alcohol problem.
- Having an alcoholic parent makes child abuse more likely.
- Around 350,000 children in the UK have a parent with a drugs problem.

Support for young carers

Many children are acting as a 'hidden army' of carers. Some experts estimate that three-quarters of all young carers are not known to social services or to teachers and others in authority.

Children are sometimes forced into caring for an ill or disabled parent because of a lack of adequate social services. Some children fear that if they seek help, they will be taken into protective care. But there are sources of help and support for young carers.

Young carer projects

Young carers should not ignore their own feelings of stress, worry or anger. It is important that they seek help before their own health and education are put at risk.

They can find out if there is a young carer project nearby. These give young carers the chance to meet and talk to others in the same situation. Some offer 'buddy programmes' for children to pair up and support one another. They can also provide practical help and advice and organize activities and outings to give young caregivers a break. Many young carers don't have time to pursue school sports or social activities that other children enjoy. They may need adult support or permission to be excused from their obligations.

Buddy schemes pair up young people who are facing similar problems and family situations.

Writing things down can be a form of therapy, as it is a way in which young people can express feelings that they might otherwise keep bottled up inside.

Dealing with feelings

Young carers have to deal with many difficult feelings and emotions. One way of coping with painful feelings is to try to write them down or express them in a poem or painting. Keeping a journal or diary may help too. Children can also learn techniques to deal with anger and frustration, such as slowing down breathing, counting down from ten to delay impulsive action, and using sport or exercise to distract and work out strong emotions.

Taking a break

Everyone in a caring role needs to take a break sometimes. Young caregivers should make sure they plan some time in the day for their own interests and enjoyment, such as listening to or playing music, participating in a sport, reading, or watching television.

In focus: online help

There are young carer websites that offer online help and information. Many have message boards where children can exchange their stories. Some organizations run telephone helplines for children to call and talk confidentially to a trained worker. They may also have online youth workers who can provide advice and information.

Chapter 5: *Family troubles*

Families can be hit hard by troubles such as debt or imprisonment. Children may feel emotions similar to those of bereavement, such as shock, loss and grief. If a child was present during a parent's arrest, the young person can sometimes experience nightmares or flashbacks about the experience. Having a family member in prison can bring feelings of shame or embarrassment, and some children can become anxious and withdrawn, feel isolated, or face bullying from **peers**. Others may have problems with grades or behaviour at school.

Living arrangements

A parent going to prison can also mean changes in family circumstances, such as financial hardship and changes in care arrangements for children. Some families have to move to a different home. When a father goes to prison, children mostly live with their mother. If a mother is imprisoned, the children are more likely to live with grandparents, other relatives, or friends. In some cases, children may need to be cared for by local authorities or placed in foster families.

Staying in contact

Some prisons will be too far from family homes to make regular visits possible, although many children stay in contact with parents through letters or phone calls. Although prison visits

Children whose father is in prison are most likely to live with their mother. They may be able to visit their father in prison.

can be stressful and upsetting, there is evidence that children benefit from seeing their parent. They are often worried about the parent's well-being, and they need reassurance that their parent loves them. Grandparents and other relatives can provide stability and care at this time.

Getting support

Because of the stigma of prison, children often feel unable to talk about their emotions. This can leave them feeling isolated and alone. Several organizations offer support for children with parents in prison. Some offer group meetings and activities so that children can meet others in a similar situation. Others offer help with prison visits, counselling, and telephone helplines that children can call for advice and information.

It's a fact: parents in prison

- 150,000 children in the UK experience a parent going to prison each year.
- Two out of three women in prison have children under the age of 16.
- 43 per cent of parents in prison lose contact with their children while inside.
- One in five children is present at the time of the parent's arrest.
- Children with parents in prison are three times more likely to suffer mental health problems than other children.

CASE STUDY

Ten-year-old Joshua was at home when his father was arrested. Josh shut himself in his room and cried for hours. He felt shocked, upset and let down because his dad had done something bad that meant he had to leave Josh and his mum. Josh didn't know anyone else whose father was in prison, and it upset him when other kids at school made remarks about his dad's imprisonment. Some of his friends called his dad names and didn't want to be friends with Josh anymore. Josh felt upset because it wasn't his fault. He was angry with his dad but still loved him and worried about what life was like for him in prison. Josh phoned a helpline because there was no one else he felt he could talk to about his feelings. A worker there put Josh in touch with a group where he could meet other children in the same situation, and that helped Josh feel he wasn't alone.

Domestic violence

Domestic violence occurs when someone hurts another member of the family. The violence can be real or threatened, and it can happen occasionally or frequently.

There are many forms of domestic violence, but they all involve someone behaving towards someone else in a controlling and aggressive way, whether it is verbal, physical, sexual, emotional or **psychological**.

Domestic violence can happen to anyone. Sometimes women are the perpetrators of domestic violence, particularly towards children or older relatives. However, most victims are women who are being abused by their husband or live-in partner. Domestic violence can sometimes be fuelled by alcohol or drugs.

Witnessing violence

Most children who live in households where domestic violence is going on are in the same or the next room when it takes place. The effects of seeing or hearing domestic violence are similar to the effects of being abused themselves. Children feel helpless and frightened and may try to protect their parent, putting themselves in danger. They can suffer many stress-related problems, including sleeplessness, anxiety and **truancy**. They may be afraid to talk about it, for fear of causing more worry and upset in the family.

Hearing domestic violence happening can haunt a child's imagination and lead to stress and anxiety. Older siblings may find themselves having to protect younger members of the family from the effects of domestic violence.

Children can also feel that it is somehow their fault that their parent or stepparent is angry and violent. This can make them feel lonely and isolated, as if they have a guilty secret they are unable to tell.

Some young people worry that they will become violent like their parent. Others may think this behaviour is normal or acceptable and start copying it. Some children start skipping school or behaving badly at school to get attention. Children sometimes abuse drugs or alcohol, or run away from home to escape an unbearable situation.

It's a fact: domestic violence

- One in four UK women suffers domestic violence from a partner at some time.
- Over half a million incidents of domestic violence are reported in the UK each year.
- Almost 2000 children ring ChildLine each year because of domestic violence.
- 44 per cent of victims reporting incidents said that their abuser had been drinking alcohol.
- In 90 per cent of cases, children see or hear domestic violence in the home.
- In 50 per cent of cases, children face domestic violence as well.

Some children who are experiencing domestic violence at home may feel unable to cope with school. They may play truant rather than face their teachers and classmates.

Getting help

When other members of the family ignore domestic violence, children are less able to cope. No child should have to cope with the effects of domestic violence alone. Women who are victims of a partner are often too scared to tell anyone or to leave an abusive partner. They may be afraid of what might happen, or they may still love their partner and hope that things will get better. Sometimes the victim may even feel responsible for the abuse. The problem may seem like a family secret, but this can give children the message that violence is acceptable or even normal.

Help available

Domestic violence should always be reported. Children can get help and advice by contacting a children's helpline or by talking to someone they trust – a relative, teacher,

Women who have experienced domestic abuse need to find a safe place for themselves and their children to stay, such as a friend's home, when they are escaping from a violent partner. They may have to leave their own home in a hurry, taking with them only the possessions they can carry.

doctor or school counsellor. They should not try physically to stop the violence themselves, because they could be hurt.

Family refuges

Many organizations provide counselling, legal help, and sometimes a safe place for a woman and her children to stay. Some children who go to live in a **refuge** with their mother may decide they don't want to see their father any more. If they do want to see their father, meetings can usually be arranged at a contact centre so that their mother is not put in danger.

CASE STUDY

Jamie often heard his dad shouting and swearing at his mum. Sometimes he heard things being thrown or smashed in the kitchen. He didn't know what to do, because when he tried to stop the fighting they both just shouted at him to get out of the room. But afterwards he could often see that his mum was bruised or bleeding.

At first Jamie didn't know what to do. No one ever talked about what was happening, and Jamie was worried that he would make things worse if he told anyone. In the end Jamie rang ChildLine because he was terrified that his mum was going to be killed. He spoke to a counsellor who told him he didn't have to go through this alone, and explained how he could get help for his mum and the rest of his family.

At many refuge centres for women escaping from domestic abuse, practical legal advice is offered free of charge. Counselling services are also available to women and children.

Bullying is a form of abuse that can become a habit within families.

Abuse

According to the World Health Organization, millions of children around the world experience abuse and **neglect** at home. Abusers can be parents, stepparents or other carers, brothers and sisters or other relatives.

The most common form of abuse is neglect, for which women are most often responsible. Neglect means not meeting a child's basic needs for food, clothes, a comfortable home, care and protection. Men are most often the perpetrators of other forms of **child abuse**, such as physical and sexual abuse.

Physical abuse means hurting or injuring someone, by hitting, slapping, beating or throwing them around. Emotional abuse is when children are not given love and approval. They may be constantly shouted or sworn at, criticized and blamed for things they are not guilty of. Sexual abuse is when a child is forced or persuaded into sexual acts

In focus: bullying in families

Bullying can happen inside families as well as in and outside school. Bullying can involve both physical and emotional abuse. Children can be bullied by parents, carers, brothers and sisters, or by other relatives. The bully can hit or push them around, call them names, constantly tease them or force them to do things they don't want to do. Sometimes, being bullied at home makes them express their anger and hurt by bullying others at school. This is often because they feel so helpless and pushed around at home, they feel the need to try and get control over others in whatever way they can.

or situations, such as touching or being touched in a way that makes them feel uncomfortable, or made to watch or take part in sexual films.

Emotional and physical harm

Bullying and abuse cause emotional harm as well as physical injuries. Children who are bullied or abused can feel worthless, powerless and alone. Sexual abuse can make children feel guilty and ashamed, and they may feel it is somehow their fault, although it never is.

Abusers will often try to protect themselves by making threats against their victims.

Feeling alone

Children often find it very difficult to talk about abuse. They may be worried they will get their parent or carer into trouble or be taken away from the family and put into foster care. They may be afraid others will not believe them. If they are being sexually abused, they may have been warned not to tell anyone else, or persuaded that what is happening is 'normal'.

Some children start self-harming because abuse has made them feel ashamed or disgusted with themselves or their bodies. Others may turn to drugs or alcohol, or run away from home.

Getting help

Children who are experiencing any form of abuse should always report it to someone they trust. This might be a relative, a teacher or school counsellor, a doctor or youth club leader. Just talking can help abused children feel less lonely and **isolated**. Childcare professionals, such as teachers and youth workers, must report the abuse so that the child receives help from the appropriate agencies.

Children who feel afraid to approach someone in person could first ring a children's helpline, where they can talk to an advisor in confidence. They will be given information and advice, and they can sometimes be given support in reporting the abuse. It can also help children to keep a diary and note down every time when they feel they have been bullied or abused.

Writing it down is a way of gaining control over what is happening, and it may also help explain to others what is happening and how they feel about it.

Taking action

When there is a report of child abuse, the police and social services may be called in. Social workers may visit the family to talk to the child and their family, and they may decide to call for a Child Protection Conference. This is a meeting to discuss problems that the child is facing at home. The people attending the conference may include family members, teachers, doctors, health workers, the police and social workers.

If the members of the social services team think that a child is in danger, they can put his or her name on a list called the Child Protection Register. Children on the register must then receive support and protection from social workers. In some cases, a child may need to be cared for by a foster family until it is safe to return home. Their

Talking about abuse can be painful and difficult, but it is important that victims confide in others. It can be helpful to keep a record of abusive incidents as a means of recalling them.

abuser may have to go to court. There are laws that can force abusers to leave the family home, and they may be sent to prison if they are convicted of child abuse. Children may find seeing their abuser in court difficult, especially if it is their father and they still love him, though they may hate what he has done. Police and social workers support children who have to go through this upsetting experience.

Children who have experiencd abuse may go to live with a foster family who can offer them support while they recover.

It's a fact:
child abuse

- 20 per cent of calls, or over 20,000 calls each year to ChildLine are about abuse.
- Most callers who report abuse are aged between ten and 15 years.
- In 2005, the Child Protective Services in the USA looked into 3.3 million reports of abuse.
- Approximately 30 per cent (28.5%) of the reports included at least one child who was found to be a victim of abuse or neglect.
- More than half of the victims were seven years old or younger (54.5%).
- More than 60 per cent (62.8%) of victims suffered neglect;
- More than 15 per cent (16.6%) of the victims suffered physical abuse;
- Less than 10 per cent (9.3%) of the victims suffered sexual abuse;
- Less than 10 per cent (7.1%) of the victims suffered from emotional maltreatment.
- During 2005, an estimated 1,460 children died as a result of child abuse or neglect.

Chapter 6: *Child runaways*

Every year, millions of children and young people run away from home. Some run away from their family. Others run away from care homes, where they have been placed because of family problems. Most runaways are in their teens, but some are as young as six years old. Many children who run away when they are very young will do so repeatedly as they get older. In some cases, they never return to their family or school.

Family problems

Most children run away because there is something seriously wrong in their lives at home. **Family dynamics** are the problem most frequently identified by callers to the National Runaway

Young people who are experiencing problems at home may be vulnerable to approaches from predatory adults on the Internet posing as friends.

Switchboard crisis hotline in the USA. Often it is caused by difficult family relationships, especially at times of crisis such as family breakup, or when a new adult joins the family. One in four children living in stepfamilies runs away by the age of 16.

Competing for attention in a new family can leave children feeling neglected and vulnerable. They may also have problems getting along with their new stepparent or siblings. One in six children living in single-parent families runs away or is turned out of home by their parent. Often their parent is finding it difficult to cope with their needs, or the young person may be in conflict with their parent's partner.

Trauma and abuse

One in four children leaves home because of physical abuse, or the threat of it. Others are being emotionally or sexually abused by a family member. Some run away because of problems with drug or alcohol addiction in the family. Children may have witnessed bullying and domestic violence, and be exhausted and stressed by constant conflict at home.

Personal problems

Some runaways are trying to escape personal problems or problems at school or with the police. Some run away because they discover that they have become pregnant, or to avoid a **forced marriage**.

Others run away because they have met someone on the Internet, and believe they can have a new life with that person. There are people who deliberately target young people, and lure them into false relationships for their own **paedophile** or sexual purposes.

It's a fact: running away

- Over 100,000 under-18s run away from home each year in the UK.
- 80 per cent of runaways run away because of family problems.
- One in four runaways leaves home for the first time while under the age of 11 years.
- One in nine children under the age of 16 runs away from home for at least one night.

Younger children are most likely to end up sleeping rough when they run away from home.

Dangers and risks

Some children run away for just a night and stay over at a friend's house. They may want their parent or carer to realize that they are unhappy, and in some way get back at them for how they feel. But others run away with the intention of starting a new life for themselves. Many children, especially runaways under the age of 11, will end up sleeping rough.

Crime and drug abuse

Child runaways face many dangers on the streets. Around one in four is homeless. They become tired, dirty, cold, hungry and emotionally drained. Their health may suffer. Many will be forced to beg or steal so that they can eat. Some turn to **prostitution** or drug

It's a fact: living on the street

- About 14,000 UK children are forced to leave home by a parent or carer each year.
- One in 14 child runaways survives through stealing, begging, drug dealing or prostitution.
- One in seven runaways suffers violence or sexual abuse while sleeping rough.
- There are between one and three million homeless children in the USA.

dealing to earn money. Runaways under the age of 16 are five times more likely to have a drug abuse problem and three times more likely to be in trouble with the police than their peers.

Children who are living on the streets can be targeted by drug dealers. Runaways under the age of 11 are most at risk of being physically or sexually abused while they are on the streets. One UK report showed that one in eight child runaways is physically hurt, and one in nine is sexually assaulted.

Young people who run away from home often have to survive on very little money and may turn to shoplifting as they cannot afford to buy food. Girls may be tempted into prostitution as a way of earning money to live on.

CASE STUDY

Finn was 11 when he first ran away from home. He was running away from constant rowing and violence between his mother and stepfather. Finn felt upset and resentful. He felt he was being pushed out of his home, and that running away was his only hope of making his own life. He caught a bus to the city and tried to find a room, but he didn't have enough money so he ended up sleeping rough. He tried begging for money at first, but it was hardly enough to survive on, so he turned to pick-pocketing and shoplifting. When he got into trouble with the police, Finn finally went home. But the problems had only got worse, and his stepfather was always bullying him and threatening him with violence. Finn ran away again when he was 14. This time, he got involved with a drug dealer, and began dealing in drugs as a way of earning money to live.

Staying safe

When children first think about running away, they may be frightened but feel they have no one in their family that they can turn to for help. There are emergency helplines that they can call to get advice and information. Social services and schools can play an important role in preventing children from running away.

Runaways are often children who have been regularly truanting, or who have dropped out of school. When children do run away, their immediate need is for a safe place to stay. They also need someone who will listen to them and take them seriously, and understand the circumstances that have led them to run away.

In focus: help in an emergency

Some projects offer emergency help for young runaways. The US project Safe Place displays signs in libraries, shops and other businesses. Where young people see this sign, they can ask an employee to call Safe Place and a volunteer will come to help counsel them and find them shelter.

Emergency shelters

There are some emergency refuges and hostels that offer young people a bed, blankets and food. Some refuges have family support workers, and offer outreach services, such as drop-in centres and street-based counselling and information, giving support, advice and sexual health care for young people.

Care and support

In some cases, children are not able to return home. They may have been forced to leave by a parent or carer, or told they cannot return, or they may be afraid of returning to problems like domestic violence and

Street-based counsellors seek out young people who are in danger on the streets and offer them information about help that is available to them.

abuse. 'Throwaway' children who have been thrown out of their home are twice as likely as others to have experienced violence in the home. They may need help from social workers to find specialist foster care. There are also some programmes that offer supported accommodation for 16- to 21-year-olds and help in getting important life and job skills. Some charities run **mentoring** and/or buddy schemes to support child runaways.

Addressing problems

Some children may be willing to return home, but need practical help and support as often they run out of money and have no transport. In the USA, the Greyhound bus line offers young runaways aged between 12 and 20 a free ticket home. If they do return, it is important that the problems which made them leave are addressed. Social services need to be aware of ongoing family conflict, and family **mediation** may be needed to help sort out differences.

Mediation can help prevent children running away again, and it may also stop younger siblings doing the same, as statistically they are more likely to run away too. There are also forums and online chat rooms where parents of runaways can meet and discuss their worries with others who have faced the same problems.

Family counselling may be needed so that all the members of the family have the opportunity to deal with the underlying problems that may have caused a young person to run away from home.

Chapter 7: *Taking control*

When a young person is having problems at home, it can be hard for them to know where to turn for help. In some cases, they may feel let down or betrayed by their parents or carers, and no longer able to trust the adults in their lives. They may be embarrassed or ashamed to tell others, or afraid of getting their parents into trouble if they seek help. But young people should not have to cope alone with problems that are making them unhappy or depressed. There are people and services they can turn to for help and advice.

Talking it over

Talking to someone they trust can help young people feel better, and enable them to think through choices or find a solution to problems they are facing. There are people they can talk to in confidence. Such people might include teachers, relatives, friends or neighbours.

Some schools have counsellors or peer support programmes, and there are other professionals who can provide support, such as doctors and youth or social workers. There are also young people's organizations that can provide support by phone or email.

Texting or emailing can be an easy way for young people to seek and receive support.

44

Personal space

Often the problems that young people face are beyond their control and this can make them feel powerless and lacking in self-esteem. Having their own 'space' and time is important so that they don't feel swamped by what is going on around them.

This can be achieved by doing activities outside the home, such as taking up a sport or hobby on their own or with friends. Even places such as parks or libraries can provide them with valuable time on their own. Some people find that keeping a diary or journal allows them to express how they are feeling, and understand the causes for their stress or depression.

But some problems will not go away on their own. Young people should

In focus: *taking action!*

If you know someone who is having a hard time because of what is going on at home, there are many ways you can give them support. Being a good listener, and letting them talk to you in confidence, without judging them, will help them.

You may also help by trying to involve them in distractions and activities, such as taking up a new sport or hobby. If you think someone is in danger, or is being abused, it is important that you tell someone you trust, so the person in danger gets the help they need.

know that there are others going through the same problems they face, and that there are people who can help them. They are never alone, whatever the family crisis. Even families that have gone through the most painful crises can heal if everyone works together.

Sport is good for physical and mental well being, and provides a useful outlet for stress and tension.

Glossary

addiction Being dependent on something so life seems impossible without it.

adopted Cared for by a parent or parents who have gone through a legal process to take responsibility for care.

anxiety Feelings of stress and worry.

arthritis A disease that inflames joints.

bereavement The loss of a loved one when they die.

binge drinking Heavy drinking of alcohol, often in one session, such as three or four drinks in less than two hours.

blended families Families made up from two separate families coming together through re-marriage or a new relationship.

bullying Acting towards someone in a way that makes them feel uncomfortable or unhappy.

child abuse Mistreating a child physically, emotionally, sexually or by neglect.

co-habiting Living together.

counsellor Someone who is trained to give advice and guidance.

custody Legal responsibility for a child.

depression The state of feeling sad and low.

domestic violence When one member of a family hurts another.

drug overdose More than the recommended amount of a drug.

endorphins Feel-good chemicals in the brain.

extended families Family units including uncles, aunts, grandparents and other relatives.

family dynamics The way members of a family interact together.

family liaison officers Officers trained to help families cope with difficult situations.

flashbacks Sudden memories of the past.

forced marriage A marriage in which either or both participants have been forced to take part, for example by the use of threats, intimidation or physical violence.

foster families Families that care for and bring up children born to other parents.

generation The time span between parents and their children.

hospices Places which offer care for the terminally ill.

isolated Feeling cut off from others.

mediation Bringing two or more people together to try to resolve their differences. Family mediation is designed to help ease conflict within families.

medication Drugs used as medicine.

mentoring One-to-one advice and guidance.

neglect Failing to care for basic needs like food, shelter, warmth.

paedophile Someone who has sexual feelings towards underage children.

paramedics Medically trained ambulance crew.

peers People of the same age group.

prostitution Selling one's body for sex.

psychological Based on the way the mind works.

refuge A safe place to stay.

self-esteem The way someone thinks and feels about him or herself.

self-harm Deliberately hurting oneself.

social worker Someone trained to help others with family or home problems.

stigma Feelings of shame caused by others.

terminal illness An illness for which there is no cure and which will cause death.

therapist Someone trained to help others overcome physical or mental problems.

truancy Missing school without a valid reason.

young carers Children or young people who take on a caring role for others.

Further information

Books to read

Kelly Bishop and Penny Trip, *Need to Know: Family Break-up* (Heinemann Library, 2004)

Andrew Matthews, *Being a Happy Teenager* (Seashell Publishers, 2001)

Kate Tym, *Coping with Families (Get Real)* (Raintree Publishers, 2004)

Andrea Willson, *Families (What's at Issue?)* (Heinemann Library, 2000)

Telephone helplines

ChildLine
A free helpline that young people in the UK can call to talk about any problems. Telephone helpline: 0800 1111

National Society for the Prevention of Cruelty to Children (NSPCC)
This charity runs a free child protection hotline which is staffed by counsellors who can offer advice and take action to protect children at risk of abuse. Telephone helpline: 0808 800 5000.

Centrepoint
This charity offers help to homeless young people over the age of 16. Telephone helpline: 0808 800 4444

Cruse Bereavement Care
This charity offers support to people who have been bereaved. Young People's Helpline 0808 808 1677

Helpful websites

www.itsnotyourfault.org
Practical information for children and young people going through a family break up.

www.divorceaid.co.uk
A helpful website about divorce with sections for children and teens.

www.thehideout.org.uk
A website for children affected by domestic violence.

www.there4me.com
A website for 12- to 16-year-olds, with information and message boards on topics including bereavement, divorce and depression.

www.youngminds.org.uk
The website of a charity that promotes the mental health of young people.

www.kidshealth.org
Lots of useful information on dealing with grief, divorce, step families, abuse and alcoholic parents.

www.winstonswish.org.uk
A website for bereaved children and their families, with practical ideas for dealing with grief, message boards and useful links.

www.youngcarers.net
Information for children who act as carers, including blogs, chat rooms and advice.

Index